# God/No-God

A Global Era Poetic Grail Quest

John Phalen

God/No-God: A Global Era Poetic Grail Quest

A Global Spirit 21 Publication

God/No-God: A Global Era Poetic Grail Quest

DEDICATION

Edward Roche Hardy

Who showed me the gateway
to the spiritual journey

God/No-God: A Global Era Poetic Grail Quest

## TABLE OF CONTENTS

### PROLOGUE

### MY LOVER IN THE NIGHT

## IT'S ALL ABOUT YOU

FOR THE EARTH AND HER LIFE CHILDREN

God/No-God: A Global Era Poetic Grail Quest

God/No-God: A Global Era Poetic Grail Quest

PROLOGUE

God/No-God: A Global Era Poetic Grail Quest

## THE ANCIENT MYTHS ARE NOT WORKING

The lines the ancients drew to connect the stars, creating myth centered pictures with stories to give them place and create meaning in their cosmos, have dissolved for us. Our modern intellect discerns an emptiness without meaning in the cosmic darkness between the stars. The No-thing preceding the Big Bang is a puzzle "out there" yet to be solved, not an awesome Mystery to be engaged. Anomie sets the mood of the time as we experience the endings of the modern social, economic and political world that shaped the lives of many of us who are struggling to find our footing in the new Global Era. But YOU whisper to us from the margins of our intuitions and we cannot deny the romantic yearning for the Beloved that beckons us at end of day.

Transcending soul is alive! Come, pioneer with me new mappings of the journey through the dark night terrors to the oasis where Plentitude blends with Void in a God/No-God Fusion. There we await Elevation to the Distant Land where we are One with YOU, Then YOU send us Homeward to serve as the agency of YOUR compassion in caring for the earth and its people.

## EULOGY

A nocturne choir of our despair
Now sings a eulogy
For ancient father gods
In symbol conscious dreams.

No heavens, no hells
Are left to choose,
No safe abode
In tribe inspired salvation rules.

What remains of Eden innocence,
Raped by scientific mind,
Can find no everlasting
World of faith
And sleeps with human ordered fate.

But hope is brother to despair
For those who dare the insanity
Of walking cosmic paths alone
Into the Silent Heart of Reality.

## I THINK, THEREFORE I AM NOT

Descartes' "I think, therefore, I am" became the "knowing" mantra of the Modern Era (15th to 20th century) reasoning that was a primary moving force in the Euro-American domination of global affairs. Reason, more what might be called technical or scientific reason, provided the genius that created modern civilization.

The brilliance of technical reason's focus is akin to a tightly beamed laser light shining through a keyhole onto the landscape of reality. What could not be observed through that focused venue of knowing was consigned to non-reality or, at least, a lesser reality. Agnosticism, as an intellectual stance for knowing/not knowing, became the positioning at the borders of this focus – a self assured denial of any reality to be known with real discretion beyond the brilliant observations of technical reason.

Sadly, the use of the term agnostic for intellectual not-knowing (via technical reason) was a misapplied derivation from the original Greek term, *agnosia,* an existential condition of experiencing unknowing. For the ancient Greeks, the term meant, as unsettling or fearful as it might be, to step into the Mystery beyond the borders of what knowing was possible through our humanly generated cognitive capacities.

God/No-God: A Global Era Poetic Grail Quest

The last century of the Modern Era, the twentieth century, saw significant challenges to technical reason's positioning at the matrix of knowing. In the century's beginnings, Freud's pronouncement of the existence of the subconscious affirmed that there was more going on in the human psyche than technical reason might be prepared to handle (try as we might). The subatomic physicists of the century seemed to challenge the tried and true rules of scientific observation through technical reason from within the scientific community itself. In the concluding decades of the century, a somewhat eclectic movement, called post modernism, highlighted, perhaps, by the rising fashions of meditation, challenged the place of technical reason as the only reliable way to explore the real.

At the same time, the brilliance of technical reason gave birth to the information technology that provided a powerful impetus to the knowing structural formation of what is now called the Global Era. It might be conjectured that the amazing new information technology of the Global Era has opened the way for relational networking to create a principal structure of human knowing, molding the deep consciousness of the child through a young adult population that must make the emerging global society their own. Subsequently any of us, especially the young raised in network relating as a daily given, experience social networking and relationship at a distance, even intimacy, as a dynamic reality not readily accessed through the observing mechanisms of laser focused technical reasoning. There is a lack of synchronicity between the mind set or deep mind structures of the Modern Era scientific observer and the Global Era relational networking consciousness being observed. At best, the focus of observations must be "fuzzy".

Some historians suggest that the world of the nineteenth century did not end until World War I. Might the global economic collapse that began in 2008 be seen as a distinctive marking of the end of the world of the twentieth century and even what is being referred to here the Modern Euro-American Era of the last five hundred years or so? The disarray in the wake of the 2008 collapse makes the increasing dysfunctions of Modern Era political, social, religious and economic systems quite apparent. The uncertainty and unknowing seeping through the seams of these Modern Era formations is the cause of anomie and a lack of affirmative will to engage a positive vision of the future.

"We're alone, it seems, alone." (see below). Those of us of the older generations, whose lives were shaped by the realities of the twentieth century, will remember the song, with it's haunting pathos, made famous by the singer, Peggy Lee, "Is that all there is." Well, the answer is no. That's not all there is.  As older generations are losing their footing in this transitional time from Modern to Global Eras, the young adult, y generation is beginning to create footings in the new, emerging Global Era. Hopefully, the newly formulating global consciousness of social networking will serve as a humanizing counterpoint to some of the harsher economic and political forces that are shaping this new era (and is it already doing so).

With the narrowly focused knowing of technical reason and the networking/relational knowing quest for intimacy at a distance taken as given parts of consciousness, the first generation of the Global Era is likely to explore the landscape of reality in some new and creative ways. Technical reason is serving them well in their continuing expansion of information technology, but it may not be seen as the primary means of human knowing - more as the enabler in a diversity of human knowing, including relational knowing. A Global Era generation spiritual genius may discover that the remarkable intimacy at a distance experienced in social networking serves as an guide for an intimate engagement with that Mystery beyond what can be perceived through the conventions of Modern Era knowing.  They may find the relationship knowing that predominates in traditional spiritualities to be a resource that resonates with their own spiritual journeys.

## God/No-God: A Global Era Poetic Grail Quest

May what follows be an encouragement for such spiritual exploration, written by one who had to leave the traditional metaphorical village when it was at the height of its influence in the twentieth century to make the journey into the spiritual dark nights   alone, with minimal support from the tradition. Nonetheless, he found himself at peace with those traditions on the Homeward Journey from the Distant Land (perhaps really seeing them for the first time.)

The following Quest for God/No-God begins in the search for the Beloved. Chuang-tzu states the matter with an elegant succinctness: "the Tao begins in the relation between man and woman and ends in the infinite vastness of the Universe." This search for the Beloved, which may or may not be realized in this lifetime, serves as respite from the dark nights quest for God/No-God.   In due course it is united with that quest. Ecstatic Oneness with the Beloved can be an integral part of the blending of Plentitude with Void in the God/No-God Fusion that is the final staging for those who are to be lifted to union with (what is called here) YOU in the Distant Land. This seeming end of the Quest is the place of departure for the Homeward Journey.  YOU send us forth as YOUR servants for the compassionate care of the earth and its people.

Having engaged the terrors of the dark night and survived them, having acquired a wisdom peace in the romantic quest for the Beloved, and having been soul united with YOU, we see the world around us with new vision. We are connected, related to YOUR earth and its people. We set about compassionate service, while poetically giving a new interpretation to the ancient term, Grail Quest for the Global Era. We find in the traditions and the ancient sacred places an affinity with those who have experienced intimacy with the Beloved and with YOU in their own terms. May what follows encourage our engagement with YOU, inspiring our compassionate service for the earth and its people.

## ALONE

Alone, it seems.
　　　　　　We're alone
In a vast cosmic sea
With our own understanding,

Technology,
　　　　　　Profound science
And a universe that overwhelms
What we can touch or see,

A sophistication that brainwashed
　　　　　　Our humanity
Tells us we are alone
With a big new future to create,
　　　　　　Progress
And a self created purpose to live

For no purpose
　　　　　　It seems . . .

Alone to cry,
"The gods are empty dreams.
　Reality's absurd
　　　　　　And love
is only passing shadows
In an uncaring cosmic sea."

Or alone to grow
And ask the question

# God/No-God: A Global Era Poetic Grail Quest

After Eden,
After Cain slew Able,
And after the American
 Tower of Babel,

Why . . .
Why we are alive
 And live
And live
And live?

Can it be
There is a final meaning to it all
In spite of entropy,
A truth
We're reaching out to touch
Alone
In the uncaring cosmic sea?

Maybe yes.
Maybe no.
But let the journey be,
A searching for the meaning
Of the why.
In the new Global Realities.

The search must live
Alone
And sometimes bend to change,

Dangerous
It seems
In these times of change.

God/No-God: A Global Era Poetic Grail Quest

But other times have known
The anguish
      Of the why
And dared darkened pathway
Of uncertainty

That we must journey now and
Be uncertain free,
      Alone, it seems.

God/No-God: A Global Era Poetic Grail Quest

MY LOVER IN THE NIGHT

God/No-God: A Global Era Poetic Grail Quest

"Who are you," she asked, "that would join with me in the mists?"

"A lone warrior, traveling in the subtle-psychic realms, looking for stories, especially love stories, that give Hope to a soul devastated world."

The way you make love is the way God will be with you.

      Rumi's variation on the Golden Rule

Where a woman and a man make love is a place holier than a church, for God is love.

      Old Russian Proverb

The Tao begins in the relation between man and woman and ends in the infinite vastness of the Universe.

      Chuang-tzu

## OPEN HANDED LOVE

Love with an open hand.
Guard against the terrible emergence
of ego expectations,
No transcending liberation there,
only haunting of dark forces.

Open handed love
Is the Wisdom navigator
For the lonely journey
To the discovery of the Beloved
And Ecstatic Union Sublime.

## IN THE MYSTERY

Finding each other in the Mystery
Where tenderness awakens Divine Knowing.
Is the surprising ecstasy we discovered here
Only to be dissolved in the "little death"
Or is it Love assurance in the now
That the alone journey into the Void
Is not all there is . . .

But wait!
Let us live this Sensuous Mystery,
Assured that the Divine Fragrances,
Awakening us to the Plentitude,
Encourage us to dwell here for a time
In the Love for which
The becoming world is mere servant.

I love you so.
I love you so.

Join with me again
In the Union of the Fires.

## NIGHT LOVERS

I am touching your soul.
I am touching your soul.
Beware!
We are entering dangerous territory.

What will happen to you in our journey,
If you come to realize the self you treasure
And want to take to heaven
Is really made for hell?

Believe it or not,
 Life will be peace centered
Once you get beyond the
Night terrors that would
Drive you away from this knowing.

And into the arms of a Love
You cannot imagine.
It is there you will discover
Who you really are.

## BEFORE THE KNOWING OF DAY

Reaching ever so tenderly
Into your last dream of the night
To engage the Ever Presence with you
That makes us one

Before this loving in the darkness
Slips behind the concealing light
Of the morning star
And we rise to the illusory knowing of the day.

## SPRING RAINS

Spring rains are creating a secluded place for us.
We don't have to scurry after sun shadows
For our private time.

Rain whispering lullabies
Ease us into loving innocence,
Letting us forget
we ate from the tree of knowledge

As I touch you in your thrilling places,
Awakening you to the ecstasy
That soon will unite us with a knowing
Where human and divine loving become One.

## LOVE'S BEGINNING

My Beloved,
I should have written our song
To the wind played melody in concert
With the night clouds dancing across the sky
As we shared love's heady wines.

God blessed us with seeing
The ancient star maps,
Guiding our souls to the place
In the sky where those of another time
Found Eternal Bliss when they died.

Could it be that the stark no-heaven
Of the present day horizontal vision
Is simply a blind spot in the modern eye?
And why so few now know the pathway
To sensually ecstatic Love Divine?

## MOUNTAIN HEIGHTS

My Beloved and I flew to the mountain heights
To see the world through YOUR Eyes.
The cosmic beyond didn't matter.
There was sufficient awe and wonder
To satisfy our souls right there,

Not only the majesty of the earth
From its heights
But more the love we shared
In YOUR Gift of Transcendent Moment
Where we knew YOU were part of us
As we became part of each other.

## DIVINE WHISPERS

The Divine Whispers at the center of soul
That awaken me would have me share
One thing with you, My Beloved.

You have blessed me, healed me
And cared for me through the kind,
Gentle spirit that is you.

And so I love you more deeply than you know
As you love me and give me strength
While I wander through the complex shadows
of a lonely and exceptional mind.

Yes, My Beloved, I love you deeply
In ways I cannot explain
Nor you can understand.

And I am saddened in the private knowing
Of who I am that I can share with only
The very, very few.

Be assured of this.
The Divine Whispers tell me
You are my Beloved in this time
And I am to await you
When I depart this earth
To journey with you into Eternity.

When it is your time.

## SOUL LINGERING

My soul lingers
In passion's "little death"
With the alone to the alone
Beckoning me
While you sleep in my arms.

I will carry our love memory,
 Soul solace in letting you go,
As I depart, a solitary traveler,
Into dawn's first light.

## OUR SECRET

There is a secret we must share.
We have companion stars that shine upon us
From the cosmic night.
GOD whispered to me
That HE made it so.

You see I know your soul,
For we were lovers in another life,
United in GOD'S Ecstasy
As you became my Beloved
For Eternity.

I love you so.
Please know
It is I who love you so in GOD'S Distant Land
When you are in dreamless sleep.
I love you so.

But now,
But now, be we separated by time and space,
You in the spring of life
And I in my winter days,
Still loving you so,

Know I will await you.
Yes, I will wait,
For our companion stars ever shine
And we will be lovers again
In another time.

## OUR TIME

I did not live the sea life this time.
But sea smells and tastes haunt me
From the soul journey of another life
That was also an adventure alone.

Today I wait in a quiet place
Beneath fragile winter sun.
I know a secret I will share.

A spring flower will awaken here
Before too long to be my companion.
And I will think that GOD is everywhere,

That there is nothing to fear
And everything to hope.
Yes, My Beloved will come to me again
 When again it is our time.

## MORNING PATHWAYS

The night bird has departed,
Leaving me in disarray
Without song in the darkness.
It is too early to expect
Guidance on the pathway into day
from the morning star.

Where is YOUR Peace
To ease my soul in the wake
Of the night bird's departure?

Has she left me forever?

There are times when knowing
Where Plentitude blends with Void
In the God/No God Fusion
For the final ascent to the Distant Land
Gives little centering preparation
For love's loneliness in this becoming world.

Please!
Let her return with the night.

## HARBINGER

A way must be found somehow
To alleviate the worries
I have to abide this day.

Does the hummingbird at my window
Have any fear for her next meal?
I know she is a harbinger
For one I loved long ago.

Ah, here is where hope is found.
My Beloved plans to return to me
This night in the land of dreamless sleep.

My deepest knowing finds peace
In this anticipation.
Yes, we are to love again.

And since our love can only be in dreamtime
While I abide the days of this life,
Might she be there to take my hand
On my last day?

Then Eternity will not be so fearful.

God/No-God: A Global Era Poetic Grail Quest

ITS ALL ABOUT YOU.

God/No-God: A Global Era Poetic Grail Quest

## ITS ALL ABOUT YOU

Its all about YOU,
Since childhood faith awakenings,
Through the artistic alchemies
Of the young man's creative dark nights,
Filled with dying gods, haunting ghosts
From past lives and other terrors,
Escaping into the Void
Where only fear made life
The choice over death,

Then the miracle blending
Of Plentitude with Void
In the God/No-God Fusion,
The Oasis for the Elevating
Journey to the Distant Land
To abide in Oneness with YOU.

Always,
It has been all about YOU

## MORNING RICHES

My soul inhales the deep riches
Of the morning solitude
Where I am awakened
 By YOUR Grace Lifting
To the pathway beyond
The last outpost
Of what we humans
Can possibly know on our own.

All yearnings quelled now,
A much longed for peace abides.
How wise YOU were
To direct me to life in the margins
Where YOU are to be known
In this way.

## A CAUTIONARY FRIEND

The ancient ones saw YOUR Hand at work
In the stillness of the stars,
 In sun, moon and earth motions,
Casting awe inspiring shadows on each other
During the extraordinary moments of their passing.

And from these mysteries of sky,
Fortune tellers discerned the fates,
Prophets interpreted YOUR Will
And shamans tried to appease YOU,
Certain that YOU were the only Liberator
From the terrors of life and death.

Such angst is diverted now
To sentimental reflection on hope past,
While we no longer dare look to sky
 For YOUR Signs, confined as we are by the
"horizontally correct" modern vision
In a culture that strives to replace
The fading metaphors that would guide us
On the ultimate journey
with the quest for sex and other addictions
We substitute for life with YOU.

But I have sought YOU
on paths away
From the leveling light of modern sky
In the margins of the knowing conventions
Where the courageous find a gateway
 Into the terrors of the night
That chase away the ancient gods and other ghosts

God/No-God: A Global Era Poetic Grail Quest

And all that is left,
All that is left
Is the dark night journey
Through the Void
To the blending
Of Plentitude with Void
In the God/No-God Fusion.

There Lifted on
   And on
     And on
To the Distant Land Beyond
And Oneness with YOU.

From there YOU have sent me back
for my final days of Peace
in the dark nights and light of day
That I might be a cautionary friend
And an encouraging teller of love stories
That engage YOU
for those who search for YOU still.

God/No-God: A Global Era Poetic Grail Quest

## TAKE HEART

Take heart, my friend and cling no more
to the myth gods of fading metaphors and stories
That can no longer give enrichment to who you are.

You will not be left soul empty in changing times.

 You are Loved at the Cosmic Source
Even when you do not believe it.

Look!

There is an eagle flying high
In the new day's beginning
Where the air is pure and clear.

## MYTHIC GARB

YOU clothed YOURSELF in mythic garb
For the ancient ones,
Allowing their intimate knowing of YOU
While shielded from the Burning Bush terrors
Of your naked Being.

But now YOU let loose these mythic garbs
In the secret shadows of knowing
For those who would dare the terrible,
Annihilating Union in the Fires

Where YOU ravish the naked soul
Of daring lovers as YOU Lift them
To Ecstatic Union with YOU,

Then depart in the silent night,
Leaving an elegant melody of Divine Joy
In YOUR Wake.

## MY MUSE

Now is the time that all things
Of my becoming world
Must be put aside,
For YOU have given me
Notice from beyond the
God/No-God dichotomy

That I must turn my feeble
Attention, be it addicted to
Becoming world illusions,
To YOUR Presence

As my MUSE in the challenging effort
To make YOU known to others
Through words.

## BEYOND GOD/NO-GOD

YOU are beyond the God/No-God dichotomy,
A cognitive "end game" of human invention,
On the journey to YOU.

Now there is no journey, no place to go,
No experience in human consciousness
That can know the All of YOU
When all is said and done.

Ah, that is dichotomy in another way,
Where I know YOU in the unknowing

And yet there is something
in the dichotomy margins,
In the whispering shadows
At the knowing/unknowing borders
That betrays YOUR Hiding.

Maybe YOU are everywhere and nowhere
And beyond it all at the same time.

## MY NIGHT SONG

The world does not hear my night song,
Composed by weaving dream harmonies
Into myth lyrics about YOU,
Prologue for the journey
Into the unknowing of dreamless sleep
Where YOU await the few.

Yes, the world dare not hear my night song.
The night bird avoids the unknowing
And  diverts a large audience
To its earthbound songs that foster illusions
 To shield a fearful world soul from night terrors.

## THE UNSEEN AUDIENCE

The ancient gods still fragrant
The substance of our souls
And shape the night vapors
Into mythic plays enacted
On the stage of our dreams.

But halt we say in light of day.
No myth plays here – so we say
In reasoned light of day.
What fools we be.
What fools we be.

We are myth driven actors,
Night or day,
In our quest to create a play
That enacts a telling story
Of why we are alive
On YOUR Stage of Reality

Where YOU are the Silent Audience
To our plays in the nights and days,
Where we pray at the dramatic moment
Before the life's final curtain call
For YOUR Applause
That tears away our actor's mask
And dissolves the ancient myths
Of night and day

God/No-God: A Global Era Poetic Grail Quest

Into the reality of YOUR Abode
Where we are truly
Who we are meant to be,
At One with YOU.

## YOU WERE NOT THERE

I looked for YOU in the quiet places
Of a harried day and YOU were not there!
YOU were not there to comfort me,

Not responding to my addictive need
For YOU to be there when I demand it!

Well YOU are a Smart YOU,
Inviting me further into the Non Presence
Where YOU are better found.

## WHO I AM

Time again to be who I am
Amidst the coffee shop customaries,
Beneath the morning Pacific gray.

Stillness is the deep ground everywhere.

Look, a gull drifting inland,
A morning food quest gone astray
Or a journey through the customaries
To the Distant Land?

## YOUR SPRING DAFFODIL

I loved YOU so,
Loved YOU so .   .   .

Ever in the journey
Through the winter's darkest night of soul,
Loved YOU so .   .   .
Loved YOU so!
(When I was certain YOU were dead!)
Loved YOU so .   .   .

But then there was the spring morning
A wayward daffodil caught my notice
For what seemed a moment!
Ah, the Eternal Moment . . .

I was admonished then for being late
In the becoming world,
Because I loved YOU so in this daffodil reprieve
From the darkest night of soul.
Loved YOU so!

And the daffodil Eternal Moment
Left hope's imprint on my soul,
Because I loved YOU so.
Loved YOU so . . .
(Even when I could not know YOU were alive!)
In the winter's darkest night of soul,

God/No-God: A Global Era Poetic Grail Quest

I could not help but love YOU so!
And now I know . . .
Now I know
The daffodil spring message,
The winter dark nights are not the end.

YOU are not lost to me
As the daffodil awakens the spring Plentitude
To unite with the winter Void
In the God/No-God Fusion,

Making me whole.

Making me whole . . .
(As I let my dead gods go.)
For the final journey to the Distant Land
Where I am One with YOU . . .
One with YOU.

And know YOU and the YOUR spring daffodil
Love me so!

## EVER YOU

I have kept my day mind
In the becoming world,
Away from YOU
Longer than I can bear.
Trying to deny my yearning for YOU.

Is it a game of hide and seek we play?

For YOUR Ever Presence never,
Never leaves me, beckoning to me
 From the day mind margins.

Ah the thirst for YOU ever with me,
Ever centered deep within my soul
Where YOU always find me .

## COMING AROUND TO WORDS

I must speak for YOU now.
Things do come around to words,
Day ending reflections
The common mind can hold on to
As soul whispers draw me
Through the night familiars
To our Union Abode.

Dare I try to speak the silence?
(As if it were possible!)
Better a farewell without regrets
To the passing day
As I turn into the night,
bound for the Distant Land.

            The night
                    YOUR Ever Night.

God/No-God: A Global Era Poetic Grail Quest

## THE EVER NOW

I did not know it was Our Time again
But YOUR shadow whispers
Call me to the Distant Land Gateway.

.

Ah, I am not one of YOUR Saints
Who ever knows YOU in the ever now.

But occasional lonely flowers
And birds in solitary flight
Do tend to my focus on YOU.

Returning me to the gift
Of loving YOU in the ever now,
Then drawing me through the terrors
Of the dark night Void
To the Plentitude-Void Blending
In the God/No-God Fusion.

And even love,
Even love of YOU in the ever now
Dissolves into the unknowing sublime
In the Grace miracle of Elevation
To the Distant land where YOU
Are YOU and I am me
And  We are One!

## YEARNINGS

Divine yearnings beckon me in the morning hours
To the deep silence where I know who I am,
Really am,
And why my life is what it is.

To Be with YOU
Is why I could do no other
Than the dark night Grail Quest,
In these Global Era times,
outside the traditional metaphorical village.

I love YOU so and know YOU
As the end of that soul journey
To the blending of Plentitude with Void
In the God/No-God Fusion
Where Grace Lifts me to the Distant Land,

Where YOU are YOU
And I am me
And We are One.

## TODAY'S JOURNEY

I love YOU so
In the quiet hour alone
When the pretense knowing
Of sense and mind dissolves
As YOUR Essence ravishes my soul.

It is more than my humanity can bear.

But I love YOU so.
Love YOU so.

Well, how shall We embrace the day?

## WILLOW WIND

Are YOU whispering to me through the willows
Or am I interrupting YOUR Night Courting
Of the murmuring brook?

No mind.
I will wait my turn,
For I know how well I will be Loved.
Memory serves me when I let it.

I will sleep a time in the quietude
Where I come to terms
With who I really am.

 And know,
And know

My Whispering Lover
Would not have me jealous of the brook.
We are at One, after all.

Awaken me
In the land of dreamless sleep
Where I know YOU so well.

Awaken me
When it is Our Time.

## WILLOW WIND 2

Is it the whisper of My Beloved
Or of YOU in the willow wind?
The night bird's song is silenced
By a Presence we both feel.

YOU are here or is it My Beloved?
It doesn't matter.
Loving YOU,
Loving her

Is the same.

## SPRING DANCE

YOUR Presence enables me to let go
My ego shadows, revealing them
As haunts without substance.

Even the spring flower knows better
Than to trust such illusions.

I wonder if I will find a naked
Dancing partner in the new sun warmth.

Of course!

It will be YOU at One with My Beloved.

## WITH YOU

I was meant to be with YOU,
The only thing I could live for,
The only thing that allowed me to live.

What will spring bring to me
After a winter too warm and bright
To be wholesome?

Winter rains have not blessed the earth
And there will be no desert spring flowers
Where beauty must sleep another year.

But I will love YOU still
And know YOU will abide the seasons with me.
We will cherish each other as always.

Love is this way.

NEVER FOREVER

I did not know it was YOU.
The night whispers are deceptive
And ghosts haunting our dreams, clever.
But YOU saved me from the loneliness
That would be mine when the morning star
Slips behind curtain of first light.

I do not want to face earth life again
But YOU assure me that YOU are with me.
I shall not die today, for YOU give me this promise,

Reminding me that Eternity is timeless now
In night or day and love only appears
To never be forever.

## MILES AND DAYS

I will return to the God/No-God
Creation Source in due time
(Be It an extension of YOU
Beyond human understanding.)

Ah, but I am One with YOU
When I pay attention
In the ever timeless moment.

(The only peace I ever know.)

Why do I wrestle with the myth gods
In my day world
And even in my dreams?

The simplest flower has the answer,
Knowing it is part
Of the ever returning spring

As the bird knows the way home
In due season
Over a course of so many miles,
So many days.

## NIGHT AND DAY

YOU must be left for a time
As I enter the day becoming world
Where I loose my footing so often.

I must name the myth gods
That haunt the shadows
Of this world, casting them out  -

First measure of the alchemy
That dissolves anomie into peace,
That day becoming may find harmony

With my night world of being
Where I know YOU so well.

## LESSER TIMES

I cannot let YOU into my day world right now.
It is one of my lesser times
When I do not want YOU with me.
Am I not to be allowed a few moments
For remorse and selfish pity?

YOU see, I loved her so,
The one I met in the wilderness
When I had lost my way
In my journey to YOU,
When YOU were dead for me,
Although I loved YOU more than
Anyone could possibly imagine.

And I thought she was all there was,
All there was about love
In those few moments of ecstasy
We shared that dissolved my despair -
An oasis of hope in the dark night of soul
Worthy indeed of a lucid dream memory
And a poem.

## YEARNING QUELLED

I love YOU so
With a yearning that cannot be quelled
By the reflected YOU known
In the quiet hour of silent meditation,
Even visiting the dark nights
Where I have a dwelling place,

For YOU are beyond my yearning,
Beyond the silence and the darkness,
Now friends, once known in terror.
Even beyond the deep subtle divine
Where the best of us worship YOU.

Come, let me be human after all
And engage a moment of joy
In an experience of earth music,
Pleased to be alive
As respite from being with YOU.

Why do I wrestle with the myth gods
That claim reality in my world,
Distracting me from the quest journey
To YOUR Distant Land?

The birds in flight know the
Essence of the Now that guides
Them through the days
And over the course of so many miles.

## COMING HOME

There are times I avoid
The mappings into subtle realms,
Becoming involved with the
Busywork of the mundane
So that I forget their guidance
Through the waste land hazards.

But then YOU get my attention
In unanticipated ways.

Indeed YOU do.

Damn, I should have been a monk
And tried to stay with YOU
All the time

But we both know
There is no salvation for me
On conventional paths.
I had to enter the dark night
Hazards alone and chart
These mappings, it seemed, alone,
Now printed in my soul.

God/No-God: A Global Era Poetic Grail Quest

And I came to know,
The mappings are the work
of YOUR Grace in the Cosmic night,

To guide me on the journey
 to the Distant Land
And YOU.

## JOURNEY TO THE DISTANT LAND

It seems I must soon leave
This world of mind clutter,
And frequently distracting trivia.

But YOU were always there for I knew
Even these twittering things were an integral
Part of YOUR Reality.

And there were occasional birds in flight off course,
Flowers growing where they shouldn't be
And at the wrong time,
Even rare stones of curious shape,
Seemingly polished for no good reason.

All of these things reflecting Extraordinary YOU
When I took the time to befriend them.
I am missing them,
These exceptional comrades
Of the crowded byways,
As I turn to the "out of town" path
That YOU kept a secret
Until it was time for me to find it.

God/No-God: A Global Era Poetic Grail Quest

And now it's time.
Yes, now it's time and YOU allow me
The pleasure of a laughing farewell
As I leave all the memories
Of the becoming world behind
For the return to the Distant Land,

There to abide for Eternity with YOU.

God/No-God: A Global Era Poetic Grail Quest

God/No-God: A Global Era Poetic Grail Quest

FOR THE EARTH AND HER CHILDREN

God/No-God: A Global Era Poetic Grail Quest

## FOR THE EARTH AND HER CHILDREN

YOU Breathed sun fire into star dust,
Creating the earth and seeding her with life,
YOUR hidden Paramour in the galactic outskirts.

And we, YOUR progeny, journey forth from her
bosom into the cosmic night
In search of her life bearing sisters
And for traces of YOUR Romantic Creation Guises
YOU use for cosmic seduction.

But the silver thread of being
That unites us with our home pulls at our
Heart as we reach the cosmic fringe, turning us
Back to see Mother Earth.

Ah the sorrow, the sorrow of the acid tears
That scar her beautiful face,
**worn by the abuse in the name of progress**
We have caused, bleeding essential being
From her breasts in grasping possession,
So that the life YOU gave birth to with her
 suffers unto death.
Oh that we might surrender the ways
 of selfish progeny to love and care
for her and the life she bears
Lest we all vanish
from the memory of YOUR stars.

God/No-God: A Global Era Poetic Grail Quest

ABOUT THE AUTHOR

John Phalen has had a diversified career as an Episcopal priest and organizer/provider of human services. He has a Master of Divinity from Berkeley, Yale Divinity School and a Doctor of the Science of Theology from San Francisco Theological Seminary. He served as an Air Force Chaplain and organized a major refugee resettlement program, then an English language/ vocational school for refugees. He is a published poet and produced playwright. Presently he is developing educational programs in Cambodia and an interfaith organization, Global Spirit 21, to facilitate Sprit engaged care of the earth and it people in the emerging Global Era.

Other works by John Phalen

Plays through Global Spirit 21/Amazon Kindle
Choir Without Song
Midnight Video
Second Sunday
Wastelands

Available through Publish America
**Poetry**
Pathways Through the Night

**Meditation Handbook**
Recovery Meditation for Gifted Misfits

www.ingramcontent.com/pod-product-compliance
Lightning Source LLC
Chambersburg PA
CBHW020601030426
42337CB00013B/1158